# AMAZING
# NATURE

Camilla de la Bedoyere

Consultant: John Farndon

Miles Kelly

# CONTENTS

◄ Perched on the edge of a waterfall, a grizzly bear carefully balances as salmon fling themselves out of the water and into its menacing jaws.

# PENGUINS
## on Parade

**T**he life of an emperor penguin demands powers of endurance far beyond our grasp. During the extremes of a polar winter, these flightless birds undertake extraordinary treks to rear their chicks and find food. They suffer starvation and endure bone-chilling blizzards in subzero temperatures.

▼ There is no nest, so the male warms the egg against a patch of bare belly skin.

▼ Up to 5,000 males huddle together, taking turns in the middle of the group where it is warmest.

### Buddy body warmth
While the females feast on fish and squid, storing energy as body fat, the males huddle together for warmth and wait. Blisteringly cold winds whip around the colony. Far from the sea, the males cannot feed, and survive on stores of body fat. It will be around 64 days until the females return.

### Meeting a mate
With little land in the Southern Ocean, emperor penguins must wait for sea ice to form in early winter before they can leave the water and set off on the long journey across the pack ice to the breeding colonies. Here they form pairs, and the female lays a single egg in mid-May. She transfers her egg onto its father's broad feet, and departs for the sea. He will care for the egg until she returns.

EMPEROR PENGUINS HAVE MULTIPLE LAYERS OF SCALELIKE FEATHERS THAT ARE TIGHTLY PACKED, SO ONLY THE HARSHEST WINDS CAN RUFFLE THEM.

▼ An emperor penguin can dive to depths of 1,300 ft (400 m), staying underwater for up to 20 minutes.

## In their element

Upon their return to the sea, the emperors' clumsy movements on land become a distant memory. Their torpedo-shaped bodies cut through the water at up to 9 mph (around 14 km/h), and they can dive to depths where there is little or no light. No one knows how the birds find their prey in deep water that is as dark as ink.

▼ Crossing vast expanses of ice is hard work, so penguins toboggan on their bellies to save energy.

## From fast to feast

The males must now undertake a journey of up to 60 mi (100 km) across the ice to reach open water. After feeding they return to the colony and from then on, both parent birds take turns hunting to feed their chick. When the sea ice begins to break up at the height of summer, the chicks and adults journey to the sea to forage.

▶ Parents protect their chicks from the extreme cold and predators, such as skuas.

## Single parents

Fully fed, the females arrive back at the colony in time for the hatching of the eggs. Each male hands over his egg and heads off seaward. When the egg hatches, the chick is fed by the mother with regurgitated food.

# LEAP of Faith

Ocean-swimming salmon head inland to breed and the sheer number of fish surging upriver makes for a captivating spectacle. For greedy grizzlies, however, this is a flying feast of fast-moving, protein-packed lunches—and an opportunity to enjoy some freshwater fishing.

## Fast food

In summer, sockeye salmon begin the journey home—they must spawn (lay their eggs) in the rivers where they themselves hatched. Knowing a feast is on its way, grizzly bears gather by rapids and falls where the salmon leap out of the water to travel upstream, or plunge into the river to trap the fish against the river floor with their giant paws. A summer diet of salmon enables a grizzly to store enough fat to survive the winter, when it may eat very little for months.

## PROTEIN PACKS

Scientists once believed there were different species of brown bear. DNA tests, however, have proved they are all the same and they share the species name of *Ursus arctos*. The variance in sizes is mostly due to the bears' diets. Kodiak bears and coastal grizzlies have access to high-protein diets.

**Kodiak**
4.5 ft (1.4 m)

**Coastal Grizzly**
4 ft (1.2 m)

**Inland Grizzly**
3.5 ft (1.1 m)

Subspecies to scale (height at shoulder)

▶ In some places, the fish are so numerous that a bear merely has to stand with its mouth open to catch a salmon as it flings itself through the air.

# Need to breed

As they travel, the salmon change from silvery blue to bright red, with greenish heads. The color develops in their skins, not their scales (which are transparent) and signifies that they are ready to mate. Ten million sockeyes may migrate up just one river in a single spawning season, turning sections of the watercourse into a cauldron of thrashing scarlet bodies. These salmon will never make the journey again—they reproduce only once in their lives.

▲ The salmon swim upstream and the females search for a suitable place to lay their eggs in the gravel, in hollows called redds.

▶ The salmon die, but their rotting bodies return nutrients to the habitat, helping to feed the fry (young fish) and other animals in the river.

## Onward and upward

The salmon hordes soldier on, but their numbers fall with every grizzly onslaught. Eventually, the survivors reach the upstream gravel beds. Females release their eggs while the males fertilize them. Soon both parents will die.

## Hatch and go

After several months the eggs will hatch, and the fry stay in the river until the following summer. As young adults they begin the reverse migration, heading downstream to the ocean.

▶ A newly hatched sockeye is called an alevin. It stays in its redd for a month, and survives on food in the egg's yolk.

# Butterfly
# CLOUDS

**M**any birds make incredible journeys, but how do tiny, fragile insects survive monumental migrations of 2,000 mi (around 3,000 km)? Monarch butterflies head south for winter, but their epic odyssey is just one part of a bizarre life cycle.

▶ Each monarch adult has a long, slender proboscis (sucking mouthpart), which absorbs liquid nectar from inside the flower.

## Generation X

Every year, the final summer generation of North American monarch adults (imagos) is different to those that came before. Instead of a short and predictable life spent sipping nectar and reproducing, these daredevils are fated to start the long journey to Mexico. As days shorten and the cool autumn air sweeps in, these imagos feed, store their energy, and set off.

## METAMORPHOSIS

Butterflies undergo metamorphosis, transforming from caterpillars into their adult form. During the summer, the caterpillars feed on milkweed, storing its toxic, milky sap in their bodies and becoming poisonous to potential predators.

1. Fat, mature caterpillars pupate. During this time of metamorphosis their bodies will develop into adults, or imagos.

2. The pupa is suspended by a silken thread. Body parts, such as the wings and abdomen, are visible on the pupa.

3. An adult emerges from the pupa. Its body is still soft and will have to harden before the imago can fly.

## A multitude of monarchs

Using the Sun as a compass and Earth's magnetic field to navigate, millions of imagos instinctively fly south. Feeding en route, the monarchs actually gain weight on their journey—possibly saving energy by gliding on air currents. They cluster together at night to rest.

▼ Countless monarchs take to the skies, traveling up to 80 mi (around 130 km) per day.

### Ready to roost

Reaching warmer roosting places is the aim of the entire journey as, being cold-blooded, the butterflies would struggle to survive the cold winters of northern areas. Imagos often select the same roosting trees chosen by previous generations, but no one knows how they do this. The Mexican forests prove to be the perfect environment for resting insects—cool enough for their metabolisms to slow down but not so cold as to freeze them.

◀ When butterflies roost they go into a form of suspended animation (a state of near inactivity), slowly utilizing their stores of body fat. Some may fall to the forest floor, others risk being eaten by birds.

▶ The monarchs' winter home was a mystery until some were tagged to monitor migrations and populations.

TAG@KU.EDU
MONARCH WATCH
1-888 TAGGING
GJE 148

### Homeward bound

Spring warmth wakens the butterflies. They become more active, and start to feed and mate. They begin the journey northward, later joined by their offspring, who complete the final leg of the migration.

# BEACH Party

**D**rawn by the light of the Moon, thousands of olive ridley turtles emerge from the sea and pour onto the shore. All turtle species come onto land to lay their eggs. But only ridley turtles lay simultaneously, in a spectacular ritual that dates back millions of years.

▼ Like all reptiles, turtles breathe air. They nest on land so that their embryos can breathe while they are developing inside the eggs.

▼ Females dig their nests at their own birthplace. They usually lay up to three clutches of eggs each year.

## Arribada!

The Playa Ostional in Costa Rica hosts up to 20,000 visiting female olive ridley turtles most months. Known by the locals as the Arribada ("arrival from the sea"), this mass appearance is an example of a smart reproductive strategy that is common in the natural world. By laying their fertilized eggs simultaneously, the females are hoping there is safety in numbers—for themselves and their young.

## Quick dig

Although they are swift-moving and agile in water, the female turtles are cumbersome on land. They haul their heavy bodies up the beach and dig a hole in the soft sand with their flipperlike forelimbs. It's hard work, and the turtles breathe loudly and deeply as they labor. The hind limbs scoop deeper to create an egg pit, and about 100 eggs are dropped into it. The mother covers her eggs with sand and, her job done, she heads back to the sea.

▼ Newly hatched turtles head for the sea. They will stay there for up to 15 years. Females remember the smell of their beach, and return to lay their own eggs.

## Hatch and dash

Baby turtles develop inside their eggs for 45 to 60 days. The ambient temperature affects their development, with lower temperatures more likely to produce males than females. When they hatch, the turtles must make a dash for the sea, avoiding any predators that lurk nearby.

▼ Fewer than one in 100 eggs hatch and the tiny turtles, with their eyes barely open, sniff the breeze and run for the sea. The run helps develop their lungs.

▼ Up to 300 people are employed to collect and sort eggs from nests at Playa Ostional.

AT ONE POINT THERE WERE FEWER THAN SEVERAL HUNDRED KEMP'S RIDLEY TURTLES LEFT. CONSERVATION EFFORTS HAVE RESTORED THE POPULATION TO 1,000 NESTING FEMALES.

## Egg harvest

Playa Ostional is the only place in the world where it is legal to harvest turtle eggs. Every year, the local community harvests about four million eggs for sale and consumption. Although the harvest is controlled and regarded as sustainable, neighboring communities appear to fare better economically by conserving their turtle nests and encouraging tourism instead.

# NATURE'S Nomads

**H**erds of wildebeest trek through African grasslands in search of food and water. Their epic journey takes them across the Mara and Gremeti rivers, where crocodiles lie in wait. The clever crocs target weak animals at the edges of the herd, so one false step could prove fatal.

## Crossing the river

The wildebeest travel in a continuous circle between the southern plains of the Serengeti and the more northerly lands of the Maasai Mara. Every year they walk for about 1,800 mi (2,900 km). These marathon migrations are punctuated by dangerous river crossings, where hordes of crocodiles gather in hungry expectation.

## Safety in numbers

In an overwhelming breeding spectacle, 8,000 calves may be be born in one day of the wildebeest calving season, which typically lasts for a few weeks between January and March. Each female gives birth to a single calf, surrounded by other wildebeest for protection. The calves vastly outnumber the potential predators—a breeding strategy that gives the herd a reasonable chance of maintaining its population size.

▲ Calves are usually born at the start of the rains, when conditions are most favorable. They are able to stand within 15 minutes of birth.

## Quickfire crocs

Most crocodiles hunt alone. Nile crocodiles, however, have learned where wildebeest cross the rivers and adapted their behavior to enjoy a feeding bonanza. They work as a group, lining up at crossing points and waiting for the wildebeest to make a move. The crocodiles identify vulnerable individuals, block their route to the shore, and close in for the kill.

▲ A wildebeest endeavors to escape the predator's jaws, but at up to 20 ft (6 m) in length, Nile crocodiles are forceful adversaries.

KENYA

Dry season

TANZANIA

Rainy season

## ROUND ROUTE

The wildebeest leave the north in the dry season, following the rains southward to calve. They return north via pastures in the west.

## Now you see me...

An estimated two million grazing animals are constantly on the move across the African grassland. Most of the migrating animals are wildebeest, but about 200,000 zebras form part of this enormous cavalcade, finding protection from lions by lurking within the wildebeest herd.

▼ Zebras can only survive by constantly moving to new grazing areas. Hiding among vast wildebeest herds provides them with cover from predators.

▲ White-bearded wildebeest are one of five subspecies of blue wildebeest. They migrate in search of food, water, and phosphorous, a mineral that the females need to produce milk.

# SARDINE
# Run

Scores of frantically working tails whisk the water along South Africa's east coast into a seething mass. Witness the sardine run—one of nature's most incredible events. This multitude of fish is a major crowd-puller and predators flock to feast here in their thousands.

▶ Cape gannets dive for fish. If they overeat they may not be able to take flight again easily, and will themselves become tasty snacks for sharks.

## Chasing currents

From May to July in most years, millions of sardines are driven by their reproductive instincts to head toward their spawning grounds. Their journey takes them northward along the eastern coast of South Africa, following cool winter water currents. Scientists have suggested that the more northerly waters provide a good environment for the sardine eggs and fry (newly hatched young) to survive—and undertaking this risky journey is a price worth paying for the better start in life it gives their young.

## Feeding frenzy

Numerous predators swim alongside the school, gradually forcing the sardines close to the shore and trapping them. Marlins, tuna, seals, sharks, gannets, dolphins, and whales are just some of the hungry hunters that come to enjoy the feast.

ALBATROSSES, PENGUINS, AND ORCAS MAY TRAVEL THOUSANDS OF MILES FROM THE SOUTHERN OCEAN TO FEAST ON SARDINES.

## Star attraction

The only defense the massive, shimmering schools have against the predators is to close ranks, creating "bait balls" to confuse them. A tightly packed swirling circle of silvery sardines distracts some animals, but the most tenacious predators are scarcely put off by this last-ditch attempt at survival. Tourists and fishermen are drawn to the spectacle, even wading into the water with nets to catch sardines—optimistic that the prowling sharks have their eyes firmly set on a fish dinner.

▼ Fishermen look for telltale signs of sardines, such as diving birds and pods of dolphins, and can land thousands of fish in one net.

▶ A sailfish uses its bill to jab at fish in the bait ball as it swims past before rushing back in to swallow them whole.

▲ Sharks are normally solitary animals but copper, dusky, bull, ragged-tooth, and tiger sharks all appear along the sardine run.

## Follow that food

The mechanics of the sardine run largely remain a mystery. A drop in ocean temperature appears to trigger the headlong rush along the coast, which explains why the run sometimes fails to occur in exceptionally warm years. The fish follow cold currents that carry huge quantities of their food, plankton, and as they swim they congregate in enormous schools, each containing millions of fish, and stretching for many miles.

# FLASH Mob!

For centuries, human ancestors believed that some animal populations spontaneously arose from dust, soil, or even rotting flesh. They had witnessed the sudden, awesome appearance of thousands of animals, with no clues as to their origin.

## Best mates

With snow still lying on the ground, the first male red-sided garter snakes waken after a winter's hibernation. The spring warmth heralds the sudden appearance of tens of thousands more, forming seething masses that wait for the emergence of the first females. This surprising spectacle is the largest gathering of reptiles in the world. As each female wakens, she finds herself surrounded by up to 50 males in a tangled heap, ready and willing to mate.

▼ An enormous swarm of mayflies takes off from the water and frenetically turns its attention to mating.

## One day

Hundreds of thousands of mayflies lurk in a pond, invisible until one special day. Surviving as nymphs hidden in the pond's sediment, the mayflies feed and grow to adulthood. A change in temperature is the most likely trigger that spurs the mayflies into action. They simultaneously change into adults with wings, and surface. In their adult form, mayflies do not even live long enough to feed—they mate and die within one to three days of emerging.

## Big babies

When millions of periodical cicadas hatch at the same time, scientists call the phenomenon a "mass emergence." But to anyone nearby this astonishing event means just one thing: a relentless chorus of raucous mating calls. The bugs survive underground for 13 or 17 years (depending on the species) as nymphs, feeding on tree roots. When their internal alarm clocks go off, the adults dig their way out and prepare to mate. The males sing to attract females, but it is a short swan song: they survive in their adult form for just a few weeks.

▼ Up to 1.5 million cicadas may emerge simultaneously in just one acre (4,000 sq m) of land to molt (shed their exoskeletons), mate, and die.

## Spooky silk

When tent caterpillars seemingly appear from nowhere, they do it in style. Millions emerge from their tiny eggs simultaneously, smothering trees and bushes with their squirming bodies. The caterpillars surround themselves with a protective shield of silk. After gorging on leaves, they return to their tents to digest their food, untroubled by birds and other predators that are deterred by the sticky silk.

◄ Caterpillars of the ermine spindle moth swarm over a tree, stripping it of foliage and leaving a ghostly memento of their presence.

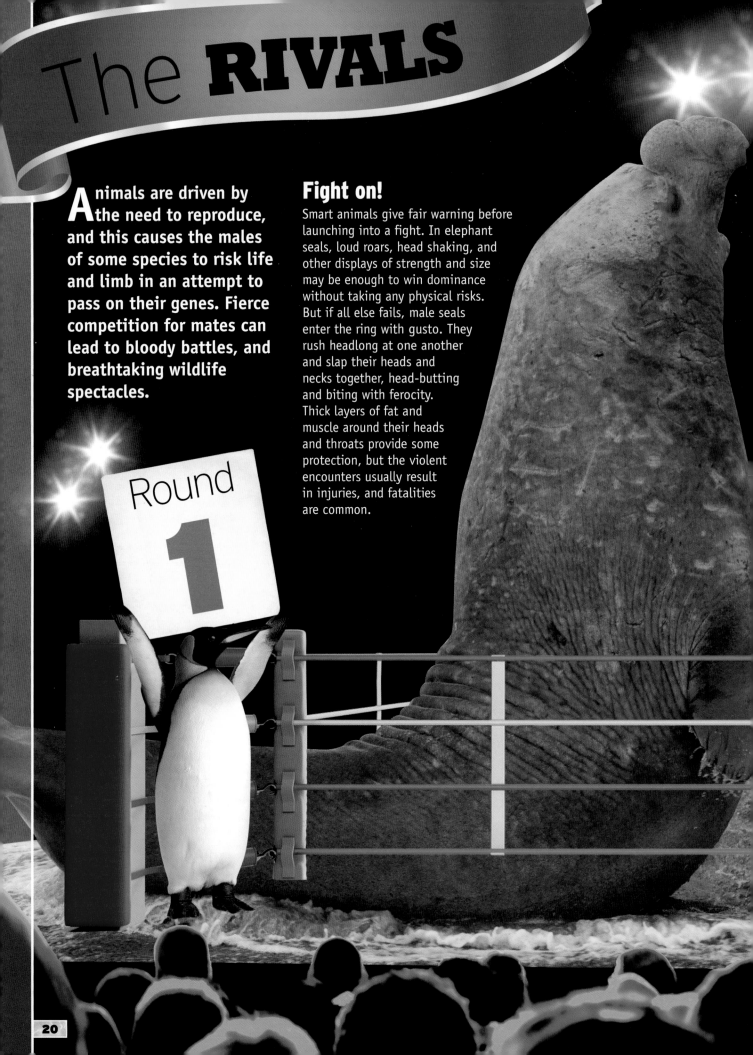

# The **RIVALS**

**A**nimals are driven by the need to reproduce, and this causes the males of some species to risk life and limb in an attempt to pass on their genes. Fierce competition for mates can lead to bloody battles, and breathtaking wildlife spectacles.

## Fight on!

Smart animals give fair warning before launching into a fight. In elephant seals, loud roars, head shaking, and other displays of strength and size may be enough to win dominance without taking any physical risks. But if all else fails, male seals enter the ring with gusto. They rush headlong at one another and slap their heads and necks together, head-butting and biting with ferocity. Thick layers of fat and muscle around their heads and throats provide some protection, but the violent encounters usually result in injuries, and fatalities are common.

Round

1

# Hercules beetle

**VS.**

# Hercules beetle

**Weapon of choice:** Giant pincer horns
**Damage:** Can slash opponent in two

**10** STRENGTH FACTOR

Regarded, for its size, as one of the strongest animals on Earth, the tropical Hercules beetle uses its pincerlike horns to grab hold of its opponent, lift it, and go for a body slam. This American mini-monster may be only 6 in (15 cm) long but it can lift 850 times its own weight. A victor wins mating rights with any female spectator.

# Giraffe V Giraffe

**5** STRENGTH FACTOR

**Weapon of choice:** Absurdly long neck
**Damage:** Rarely fatal

Adult male giraffes living in small groups frequently spar with one another, especially when fertile females are around. Known as necking, they fight by walloping their necks against each other and using their heads like clubs. A well-timed swing can knock an opponent to the ground, leaving it temporarily unconscious.

◄ When male elephant seals fight, they inflate their noses and roar. Their roars are so loud they can be heard from miles away.

# SPANISH IBEX

**8** STRENGTH FACTOR

# SPANISH IBEX

**Weapon of choice:** Huge horns
**Damage:** Serious flesh wounds may lead to death

Dueling is common in horned animals, but male Spanish ibex are gladiators without equal. Male battle for mating rights, relying on their tough skulls and muscle-packed shoulders for defense during fights, known as "ruts." Despite this protection, horns that grow to 26 in (75 cm) length can deliver deadly wounds.

# SO MACHO

In the animal world, it is not uncommon for males to try to mate with as many females as possible. To do so they may have to fight off other males, and in these instances great strength, size, and weapons are an advantage. As a result, the males of some species grow to be enormous compared to females, and often labor under impressive horns or antlers, have immensely muscular shoulders, or possess outsize fangs and claws.

▲ A male elephant seal can weigh four or five times as much as a female.

# Think PINK

**S**hocking pink flamingos flock to Africa's soda lakes, strutting and gliding across the rich waters. More than one million lesser flamingos arrive to feed and dance, and create what is regarded as one of the world's most beautiful sights.

## Dazzling dancers

Millions of pink flamingos arrive at a soda lake to prepare for their extraordinary courtship dances. They begin by flicking their heads and flapping their wings, but soon move into a synchronized parade. Groups of marching flamingos meld into larger congregations that move so smoothly through the water that they appear to be gliding or skating. Eventually—no one knows how—pair bonds begin to form and nesting soon follows.

## Soda soup

A number of soda lakes line the Great Rift Valley in Africa. The blistering heat and a high concentration of alkaline minerals in the water have created basins of caustic soda that are hostile to most forms of life. However, tiny life forms called cyanobacteria can thrive here. The population of one type, *Spirulina*, periodically explodes and turns the water to a thick, nutritious, pea-green "soup." It is favored by flamingos, which gather in large numbers to feast on a bumper crop.

▶ Tens of thousands of flamingos can descend on Kenya's Lake Bogoria at a time.

# Flame birds

Flamingos are named from the Latin word *flamma*, or flame. Their extraordinary color comes from *Spirulina*, which contain carotenoid pigments. The flamingos eat the cyanobacteria and the pigments are transferred to their feathers. To feed, flamingos use their large feet to stir the water, bringing the *Spirulina* to the surface. Then they swing their heads, upside down, from side to side. Inside their mouths are thousands of thin plates that strain the tiny organisms from the water.

▼ Even while feeding, flamingos are able to keep a watchful eye open for predators.

◄ During their courtship dances, groups of male flamingos break up, reunite, and change direction simultaneously.

## DANGER AHEAD!

Africa's lesser flamingos are declining in number because their soda lake ecosystems are threatened. Commercial extraction of soda ash from the lakes damages the habitat, but growing populations of people around the lakes are also having a significant impact. More water is being drawn from the rivers that feed the lakes for agricultural use, and pollution entering the lakes is on the rise.

▲ Hyenas run alongside the lake, hoping to get lucky and grab a bird as it takes off.

# SWARM!

A single swarm of 20 million bats may seem a frightening prospect, but these small flying mammals are helpful, not harmful. Mexican free-tailed bats form some of the greatest congregations of animals on Earth, and tens of millions may inhabit just one cave. These colonies need an enormous quantity of food to survive, and their diet is made up entirely of insects, many of which are agricultural pests.

## NIGHT FRIGHT

### THE FLAPPING HORDES LEAVE THEIR ROOST TO HUNT

## Invasion of the KILLER BEES

To the untrained eye, an Africanized or "killer" bee looks just like a European honeybee. Killer bees, however, are very aggressive, and quick to swarm when food is scarce, or when they want to create new nests. Swarms can detect people 50 ft (15 m) away from their nests and don't hesitate to sting in defense. They move swiftly to attack, and will even chase people some distance. While one sting is rarely fatal, hundreds of stings can prove to be lethal.

**T**HE ACTIONS OF A SINGLE BEE, BIRD, BAT, OR BUG MAY APPEAR INSIGNIFICANT, BUT WHEN SPECIES BAND TOGETHER THEY CAN PUNCH FAR ABOVE THEIR WEIGHT AND HAVE A DRAMATIC IMPACT. THE MOST AWESOME SWARMS NUMBER MILLIONS OF INDIVIDUALS, AND MAKE FOR A SPECTACULAR SIGHT.

A TAWNY MASS HOVERS AND SWIRLS OVER THE AFRICAN SCRUBLAND...

# PHENOMENAL FLOCKS

From a distance it could be mistaken for a fast-moving dust cloud, but a closer look reveals that it is actually a congregation of the world's most abundant bird—the red-billed quelea.

Thousands of these weaver birds flock to feast on seed crops and trees, stripping them bare. There are more than 1.5 billion red-billed queleas in total, and some flocks are so huge they can take five hours to pass overhead.

**A SWARM OF LOCUSTS MAY NUMBER 16,000,000,000 INDIVIDUALS!**

# LOCUST PLAGUE!

## WHEN THE POPULATION OF LOCUSTS IN AN AREA OUTGROWS THE AVAILABLE FOOD, IT'S TIME TO SWARM. . .

- A locust eats its bodyweight in food every day.
- A swarm can devour 35,000 tons of food in 24 hours.
- In 2004, around 69 billion locusts gathered in a mega-swarm, devastating parts of northwest Africa.
- A swarm can travel 80 mi (around 130 km) or more in one day.
- One long-distance migration in 1988 saw locusts travel from West Africa to the Caribbean—that's about 3,000 mi (nearly 5,000 km) in ten days.

▶ In 2004, Senegal suffered one of the world's worst locust invasions.

# Marine Marvels

Some of nature's most awesome events occur beneath the surface of the sea and at its coasts. Hidden from human eyes, convoys of lobsters march across the seabed, while blooms of golden jellyfish gently propel themselves through salty waters, and colorful squid dance for their mates.

## Golden jellies

Up to ten million golden jellyfish migrate in the marine lakes at Palau, in the Pacific Ocean. The saline lakes are enclosed, but still experience tidal flows because ocean water has access to them. Every morning, the jellyfish move up to the surface of the water and swim across the lake, following the course of the Sun. Sunlight is essential for the health of the algae that live inside the jellyfish and provide them with energy.

## Flash dance

The Australian giant cuttlefish grows to 5 ft (1.5 m) in length. In winter, many thousands migrate to shallow waters where the males dazzle females with spectacular displays of color. The dances begin with a show of size, as the males stretch out their "arms" to prove their superiority, and zebra patterns whizz down their flanks. Like other cuttlefish, these giants can change color in an instant, and they produce a show so impressive that divers, as well as female cuttlefish, gather to enjoy the performance.

▼ A male broadclub cuttlefish shields his mate from a potential rival during their courtship ritual.

## Quick march

Late summer storms spur Caribbean spiny lobsters into action. As their coastal waters cool, and low winds make the shallow waters murky, the lobsters get ready to move. Lined up in single file, the intrepid crustaceans march to deeper areas, where warm water speeds the development of the females' eggs. They will mate here, and return to the shallows in spring.

▲ Each spiny lobster touches the tail fan of the lobster in front as it walks, forming an orderly line. It's a bizarre event, and one which few people ever witness.

▼ Golden jellyfish bask in sunlight so that the microscopic algae that live inside them have access to the light rays they need to survive.

## Land ahoy!

When a killer whale approaches an ice floe or land, there is little warning other than the sudden appearance of its black dorsal fin. Also known as orcas, these super predators come in search of a meaty seal takeaway. Using enormous strength and speed, orcas fling themselves onto shore to grab their prey. When a seal is resting on ice floes, an orca can tip the frozen slab, so lunch almost rolls into its mouth!

▶ An orca, despite its huge bulk, heaves itself onto shore, surprising a sea lion that has no time to escape.

SPINY LOBSTERS MIGRATE UP TO 30 MI (ABOUT 50 KM) IN A FEW DAYS. BY WALKING IN SINGLE FILE THEY REDUCE DRAG, SO THEY CAN MARCH AT DOUBLE-QUICK TIME!

# NONSTOP Godwits

**M**any birds undertake phenomenal journeys during their seasonal migrations, but bar-tailed godwits are the most awesome of all aviators. They embark on epic nonstop journeys that take them halfway round the world.

## Globetrotters

Godwits are wading birds, with an unremarkable appearance that belies their incredible stamina. They reside in the cool tundra regions of the north, where they nest and raise their chicks in summer. The birds then move southward to feed and stock up their body fat until it constitutes more than half of their bodyweight. They can then fly nonstop southward, crossing the Equator to reach feeding grounds.

## Extreme endurance

Godwits migrating south never rest, eat, or drink, even though some of them are just two months old. As winter approaches in the Southern Hemisphere, the birds prepare for the return journey. Some of them may stop off in Europe en route, to enjoy milder weather than that endured by the birds that make it back to the tundra.

▶ This muscular male godwit is leaving Norway. His ultimate destination will be Australia, New Zealand, or South Africa.

## The record-setter

A female godwit known as E7 was tracked undertaking the longest, fastest nonstop migratory flight in the world. After leaving New Zealand in March 2007, E7 stopped in China to rest and feed. She then flew onward to Alaska, where she raised two chicks. On August 29, E7 left for her nonstop journey back to New Zealand, and reached her feeding grounds in just eight days.

Alaska (U.S.)

CHINA

PACIFIC OCEAN

1–15 May
4,500 mi (7,237 km)

29 Aug – 7 Sept
7,200 mi (11,570 km)

17–24 March
6,340 mi (10,219 km)

Start/Finish

NEW ZEALAND

## RED KNOT PIT-STOP

Red knots achieve a similar long distance feat to bar-tailed godwits, migrating between the southerly parts of South America and the Canadian Arctic. Each journey covers about 10,000 mi (17,000 km). They make pitstops on the way to feed and rest, but the most spectacular of these coincides with the mass arrival of horseshoe crabs at Delaware Bay in North America. The arthropods congregate to mate, and their eggs are perfect packets of protein and energy.

▲ Hordes of hungry birds, including red knots, descend on Delaware Bay, and spend several weeks gorging on horseshoe crab eggs.

## SEA SWALLOWS

Arctic terns don't care that the shortest distance between two points is a straight line. Their remarkable migration between the Poles follows a figure-of-eight pattern that adds several thousand miles to their journey. The detour makes sense, because it allows the terns to save energy by traveling on the prevailing wind. Every year, a tern may fly 43,000 mi (70,000 km).

▼ Arctic terns are sometimes known as sea swallows, because of their aerobatic skills, and stamina in the sky.

ARCTIC TERNS CAN LIVE FOR UP TO 20 YEARS. ONE BIRD MAY FLY MORE THAN 200,000 MI (322,000 KM) IN ITS LIFE—THAT'S EQUIVALENT TO FLYING FROM EARTH TO THE MOON.

# BLOOMING Brilliant

**P**lants operate on a different timescale to animals and most reproduce, feed, and breathe without making any obvious movements or undergoing large changes. So when awesome events happen, they are especially momentous.

▲ As a titan arum flower grows it emits a nauseating smell. Its top tip eventually reaches a height of up to 10 ft (3 m) above the ground.

## Sudden stench

The flowering of the stinky titan arum is unpredictable but when it happens, the event is spectacular. The tropical plant produces a massive flowering structure (called an inflorescence) from a tuber that weighs 150 lb (70 kg) or more—it's the largest tuber in the plant kingdom.

◀ The thick, leathery Rafflesia petals unfurl overnight, into a flower that measures up to 42 in (107 cm) across.

## Corpse flower

The Rafflesia is said to smell of rotting flesh, but it is better known for its looks—it grows unobtrusively before erupting into the world's largest flower. However the blooming is unpredictable, and each flower lasts only a few days. Rafflesia grows as a parasite on rain forest vines and relies on small flies to pollinate its flower.

## Fig feast

When a giant fig tree produces its fruit, there are rich pickings for everyone. Since these trees only fruit once every two years, the inhabitants of its Indonesian rain forest home turn up in their droves to eat their fill, including long-tailed macaques, red leaf monkeys, orangutans, gibbons, and thousands of birds. For a short while the tree becomes the hub of a noisy feasting crowd, and after a few weeks the bonanza is over.

◀ A gray gibbon swings between the branches of a fig tree to dine on its juicy fruits.

BAMBOO SHOOTS CAN GROW MORE THAN 12 IN (AROUND 30 CM) IN A SINGLE DAY, AND MAY REACH 100 FT (ABOUT 30 M) IN A SINGLE GROWING SEASON.

## Burst into bloom

Bamboo forests are formed from tall-growing grasses, and once every 30 to 40 years a unique phenomenon, not yet understood by scientists, sweeps through them. It is a process called masting, when all the bamboo plants of one species spontaneously burst into flower over a large area. All the plants then simultaneously die.

▼ Giant pandas feed on bamboo. They feast during a masting event, but then face starvation when an entire bamboo forest dies afterward.

▲ Flies are trapped, turned into a tasty soup by digestive juices, and then absorbed by the plant.

## Meat eater

Hidden in the boggy undergrowth in North or South Carolina, U.S., the Venus flytrap is easy to overlook. But a keen eye and great patience can be greatly rewarding: these plants are killers. Unlike most plants they do not make their food—they eat it. Their sensitive leaves form traps, and when a fly crawls inside, they respond by snapping shut—as fast as the blink of an eye.

# Catch the KILLER

The natural world is a dangerous place, where death may be just around the corner. When a predator goes in for a perfectly timed attack on its prey, the task of grabbing a meal becomes a dazzling natural spectacle.

## Stoop and scoop

The moment when a peregrine falcon turns a hover into a stoop (power-dive) is so sudden that catching sight of it is a rare privilege for any wildlife watcher. These raptors are the fastest animals in the world, but they owe their hunting prowess as much to the accuracy of their eyesight as to their speed. A stoop brings the predator toward its aerial target at estimated speeds of over 200 mph (about 320 km/h).

**TOP SECRET**

▼ With forward-facing eyes, a peregrine can focus on its prey even while in a vertical dive.

## Squeeze me

Some snakes take their time over lunch, and are prepared to wait weeks between meals. When the opportunity to feed arises, however, constrictor snakes are swift to strike. Once a python or boa has gripped the prey in its jaws, it wraps its huge, muscular coils around the body and slowly squeezes. This death grip forces all the air from the prey's lungs until it suffocates.

▲ A rock python can open its jaws wide enough to engulf the body of a ground squirrel.

## Going in for the kill

Solitary big cats rely on stealth, speed, and strength to kill. Yet while they are supreme predators, their prey has also evolved ways to stay alive, relying on alertness, speed, and a dogged determination to survive. As many as three out of four cheetah hunts are unsuccessful, and some tigers fail to make a kill 90 percent of the time they pursue prey.

► A cheetah keeps its prey in its sights as it stalks to within sprinting distance.

## Pack attack

Like many hunters, wolves often hunt under the cover of dark. Their natural forest habitats provide extra cover, and help these carnivores to remain hidden from even the most alert prey. Wolves usually hunt as packs of up to eight family members, and a successful hunt requires great coordination between all individuals.

▲ The alpha (dominant) pair of wolves feed first. The other pack members are only allowed to join in when the appetites of the alpha pair are sated.

## Tongue tricksters

A chameleon's lightning-quick attack is so speedy that it is almost impossible to catch with the naked eye. The reptile's super-sticky tongue catapults out of its mouth at 13.4 mph (21.6 km/h), and accelerates from 0 to 20 ft (0 to 6 m) in 20 milliseconds. Even flies, which have lightning-quick reactions, are too slow to escape.

► The tip of a Madagascan parson's chameleon's tongue works like a small suction cup.

# ONE YEAR

## IN THE WILD

**E**very minute of every day, extraordinary events occur in the natural world. Driven by the instinct to survive, there is always an awesome spectacle to be seen somewhere. Follow a selection of nature's highlights around the globe and be amazed from January to December.

## January

Many hundreds of bald eagles gather at their winter habitat at Klamath Basin marshes in Oregon, U.S. These majestic birds spend the coldest months of the year on the frozen water, feeding on waterfowl.

## April

Two million migratory birds gather around Broome in Western Australia to begin their 6,000 mi (10,000 km) flight to the Northern Hemisphere, along the Australasian flyway— one of the world's greatest migratory flight paths.

## May

A four-hour trek through drizzle and high vegetation in the Rwandan cloud forest may be rewarded with the sight of a family of endangered mountain gorillas. Some have become accustomed to human presence, and will continue to play and eat while spectators watch.

## August *

The Danum Valley in Borneo is hard to reach, but the trip deep into a rain forest is worthwhile. Watch orangutans in the wild while you can—they face extinction within 20 years because their habitat is being replaced by palm oil plantations.

## September

*Wish You Were Here!*

Male elks in Yellowstone National Park, Wyoming, U.S., begin the rutting season. Furious fighting precedes mating.

## October

## February

Whale sightings are at their best in the Southern Hemisphere's summer. Minke, humpback (left), beaked, fin, southern right, and blue whales can be spotted around the Antarctic Peninsula and into the Southern Ocean. They come to feast, making the most of a temporary abundance of food.

## March

Tigers are one of the world's most elusive big cats, and this is a good time to see them in the Sunderban and Ranthambore Tiger Reserves in India.

## June

Sloth bears in Sri Lanka are normally nocturnal, but in June they become active in the day as well, so they can feast on the trees' ripening fruit.

## July

The glorious purple emperor butterfly is an elusive woodland inhabitant. This is the best time to see it flying around the U.K.'s native oak trees.

Only the males have the resplendent purple sheen, which is created when light is refracted by the wing scales. Females are brown.

## November

On clear mornings by the upper Tambopata River in Peru, hundreds of macaws arrive to lick clay from the bank. Eating earth is called "geophagy," and it occurs in several animal species. The clay contains minerals that may be useful supplements to an animal's diet.

Thousands of polar bears gather at Churchill, Manitoba in Canada. They are waiting for the Hudson River to freeze over so they can hunt.

## December

In Japan, China, and Russia, Japanese red-crowned cranes gather to begin their beautiful, synchronized courtship dances.

# On the HOOF

**P**ronghorns and caribou undertake the longest migrations of any land animals in the New World. Long ago, there may have been millions of these deer trekking across the North American plains, but interference from humans has added many obstacles to their journeys.

## Going the distance

Caribou herds may number thousands, and make 3,000-mi (about 5,000-km) journeys through the course of a single year as they move to find better grazing areas, to calve, and to avoid the winter's worst weather and the summer's biting insects. Caribou can be flexible in their routes, so one year's migration might differ in route and distance from the previous year's, and may involve crossing water as well as land. Caribou can swim very well, and their winter coats have hollow hairs, which help the deer to float high in the water.

## Following the food

Further north, vast herds of caribou conduct their migrations with much less interference from people. Also known as reindeer, these hoofed mammals trek through the Arctic tundra and boreal regions, where food and humans are scarce, although caribou territories once extended much further south.

▶ Caribou from the Porcupine Herd forge onward in Alaska. Their progress is tracked by satellite so that scientists can document their migratory patterns.

▼ Bison are now being allowed to exercise their migration instincts. Until recently they were confined to national parks, such as Yellowstone in Wyoming, U.S.

## Buffalo woes

Yellowstone National Park, in Wyoming, U.S., is home to one of the largest free-roaming herds of bison (also known as "buffalo"). They are direct descendants of the 30 million bison that once populated the Great Plains, before relentless hunting saw their numbers fall to just 1,091 in 1889. Efforts to conserve bison often fail when the animals' instinct to migrate puts them into conflict with farmers.

◄ Many caribou migration routes require the herds to cross sizeable rivers.

▼ Pronghorns cross busy roads and squeeze through barbed wire fences to reach their summer home.

## Obstacle course

There are about half a million pronghorns in Wyoming, U.S.—about the same as the number of people. But almost 80 percent of the animals' ancient routes between winter feeding and summer calving grounds have disappeared beneath commercial developments. Now only one herd makes the seasonal journey, and the 100-mi (160-km) route tests the pronghorns' endurance to the limit. The natural landscape has been broken up by urbanization and roads to such an extent that reaching the calving ground is now an unnaturally hazardous exercise.

# ELEPHANTS
## on the March

**E**lephants walk with intent when they are on the move. Driven by the need for water and food, a herd on the march creates a majestic procession that seems to operate with a single mind. These extremely intelligent animals are highly social and have strong family bonds.

ELEPHANTS CAN COMMUNICATE WITH EACH OTHER BY MAKING LOW-FREQUENCY RUMBLES. THE SOUNDS PASS THROUGH THE GROUND TO HERD MEMBERS, WHICH HEAR THE RUMBLES THROUGH THEIR FEET.

▼ As the length and severity of droughts in parts of Africa increase, herds of desert elephants spend their days wandering in search of water.

## BIG APPETITES

An adult elephant needs to eat 350 lb (160 kg) of food every day, and may tear down branches to get fruit, strip bark, and even fell whole trees to feed. When a herd of these huge animals is confined to a small area it can inadvertently demolish its own food source, which is why elephants need massive territories, and many of them migrate to survive.

## DROUGHT AND DEATH

The search for water is a powerful motivator in arid regions of Africa. During the dry seasons, river courses become dusty tracks of rubble and sand for months on end, so elephants must endure blistering heat, dust storms, and near starvation to reach the ever-dwindling waterholes.

▶ Elephants use their trunks to reach deep into waterholes in search of water. They may also find sodium in the water and surrounding rock. This essential mineral is lacking in the diet of many elephants in arid areas, so they eat soil or lick rock to get it.

▼ Elephants follow safe routes between waterholes and neighboring national parks and tourists congregate to view the spectacle.

## ON THE RIGHT ROAD

The future is looking good for Namibia's migrating elephants—the largest elephant population in Africa. Since the value of the herds to the ecosystem and tourism has been appraised, conservation has been put high on the national agenda. Corridors—the pathways followed by migrating elephants—are now protected. Elephants in different areas face different problems, so conservation efforts have to be tailor-made to fit each region.

TEMPERATURES SOAR TO 120°F (49°C) IN MALI'S SAHEL REGION, WHILE ELEPHANTS COMPLETE ROUND TRIPS OF 300 MI (480 KM) EVERY YEAR TO FIND WATER AND FOOD.

▼ Up to ten African elephants descend on this Zambian lodge every October when the mango trees fruit. The hotel now encourages guests to enjoy the spectacle.

## ELEPHANT IN THE ROOM

When hotels are built on ancient elephant corridors, the animals do not always understand that they should take a detour. A herd of elephants was not deterred by the erection of Mfuwe Lodge at South Luangwa National Park in Zambia— they simply walked right through the hotel's reception to reach the fruiting mango trees they have been visiting for generations.

# INDEX